The award-winning pictures gathered in this diary have been drawn from the archives of the Wildlife Photographer of the Year competition – the international showcase for the very best nature photography. The competition is owned by the Natural History Museum, London, which prides itself on revealing and championing the diversity of life on Earth.

Wildlife Photographer of the Year is one of the most popular of the Museum's exhibitions. Visitors come not only to see breathtaking imagery, but also to understand some of the threats faced by our planet's animals and plants. Understanding and finding ways of conserving the Earth's biodiversity is at the heart of the Museum's work. This exhibition is one way to share that mission with others, encouraging us to see the environment around us with new eyes.

The Natural History Museum looks after a world-class collection of over 80 million specimens. It is also a leading scientific research institution, with ground-breaking projects in more than 68 countries. About 200 scientists work at the Museum, researching the valuable collections to better understand life on Earth. Every year more than five million visitors, of all ages and levels of interest, are welcomed through the Museum's doors.

2019

JANUARY

wk	M	T	W	Th	F	S	S
1		1	2	3	4	5	6
2	7	8	9	10	11	12	13
3	14	15	16	17	18	19	20
4	21	22	23	24	25	26	27
5	28	29	30	31			

FEBRUARY

wk	M	T	W	Th	F	S	S
5					1	2	3
6	4	5	6	7	8	9	10
7	11	12	13	14	15	16	17
8	18	19	20	21	22	23	24
9	25	26	27	28			

MARCH

wk	M	T	W	Th	F	S	S
9					1	2	3
10	4	5	6	7	8	9	10
11	11	12	13	14	15	16	17
12	18	19	20	21	22	23	24
13	25	26	27	28	29	30	31

APRIL

wk	M	T	W	Th	F	S	S
14	1	2	3	4	5	6	7
15	8	9	10	11	12	13	14
16	15	16	17	18	19	20	21
17	22	23	24	25	26	27	28
18	29	30					

MAY

wk	M	T	W	Th	F	S	S
18			1	2	3	4	5
19	6	7	8	9	10	11	12
20	13	14	15	16	17	18	19
21	20	21	22	23	24	25	26
22	27	28	29	30	31		

JUNE

wk	M	T	W	Th	F	S	S
22						1	2
23	3	4	5	6	7	8	9
24	10	11	12	13	14	15	16
25	17	18	19	20	21	22	23
26	24	25	26	27	28	29	30

JULY

wk	M	T	W	Th	F	S	S
27	1	2	3	4	5	6	7
28	8	9	10	11	12	13	14
29	15	16	17	18	19	20	21
30	22	23	24	25	26	27	28
31	29	30	31				

AUGUST

wk	M	T	W	Th	F	S	S
31				1	2	3	4
32	5	6	7	8	9	10	11
33	12	13	14	15	16	17	18
34	19	20	21	22	23	24	25
35	26	27	28	29	30	31	

SEPTEMBER

wk	M	T	W	Th	F	S	S
35							1
36	2	3	4	5	6	7	8
37	9	10	11	12	13	14	15
38	16	17	18	19	20	21	22
39	23	24	25	26	27	28	29
40	30						

OCTOBER

wk	M	T	W	Th	F	S	S
40		1	2	3	4	5	6
41	7	8	9	10	11	12	13
42	14	15	16	17	18	19	20
43	21	22	23	24	25	26	27
44	28	29	30	31			

NOVEMBER

wk	M	T	W	Th	F	S	S
44					1	2	3
45	4	5	6	7	8	9	10
46	11	12	13	14	15	16	17
47	18	19	20	21	22	23	24
48	25	26	27	28	29	30	

DECEMBER

wk	M	T	W	Th	F	S	S
48							1
49	2	3	4	5	6	7	8
50	9	10	11	12	13	14	15
51	16	17	18	19	20	21	22
52	23	24	25	26	27	28	29
53	30	31					

2020

JANUARY

wk	M	T	W	Th	F	S	S
1			1	2	3	4	5
2	6	7	8	9	10	11	12
3	13	14	15	16	17	18	19
4	20	21	22	23	24	25	26
5	27	28	29	30	31		

FEBRUARY

wk	M	T	W	Th	F	S	S
5						1	2
6	3	4	5	6	7	8	9
7	10	11	12	13	14	15	16
8	17	18	19	20	21	22	23
9	24	25	26	27	28	29	

MARCH

wk	M	T	W	Th	F	S	S
9							1
10	2	3	4	5	6	7	8
11	9	10	11	12	13	14	15
12	16	17	18	19	20	21	22
13	23	24	25	26	27	28	29
14	30	31					

APRIL

wk	M	T	W	Th	F	S	S
14			1	2	3	4	5
15	6	7	8	9	10	11	12
16	13	14	15	16	17	18	19
17	20	21	22	23	24	25	26
18	27	28	29	30			

MAY

wk	M	T	W	Th	F	S	S
18					1	2	3
19	4	5	6	7	8	9	10
20	11	12	13	14	15	16	17
21	18	19	20	21	22	23	24
22	25	26	27	28	29	30	31

JUNE

wk	M	T	W	Th	F	S	S
23	1	2	3	4	5	6	7
24	8	9	10	11	12	13	14
25	15	16	17	18	19	20	21
26	22	23	24	25	26	27	28
27	29	30					

JULY

wk	M	T	W	Th	F	S	S
27			1	2	3	4	5
28	6	7	8	9	10	11	12
29	13	14	15	16	17	18	19
30	20	21	22	23	24	25	26
31	27	28	29	30	31		

AUGUST

wk	M	T	W	Th	F	S	S
31						1	2
32	3	4	5	6	7	8	9
33	10	11	12	13	14	15	16
34	17	18	19	20	21	22	23
35	24	25	26	27	28	29	30
36	31						

SEPTEMBER

wk	M	T	W	Th	F	S	S
36		1	2	3	4	5	6
37	7	8	9	10	11	12	13
38	14	15	16	17	18	19	20
39	21	22	23	24	25	26	27
40	28	29	30				

OCTOBER

wk	M	T	W	Th	F	S	S
40				1	2	3	4
41	5	6	7	8	9	10	11
42	12	13	14	15	16	17	18
43	19	20	21	22	23	24	25
44	26	27	28	29	30	31	

NOVEMBER

wk	M	T	W	Th	F	S	S
44							1
45	2	3	4	5	6	7	8
46	9	10	11	12	13	14	15
47	16	17	18	19	20	21	22
48	23	24	25	26	27	28	29
49	30						

DECEMBER

wk	M	T	W	Th	F	S	S
49		1	2	3	4	5	6
50	7	8	9	10	11	12	13
51	14	15	16	17	18	19	20
52	21	22	23	24	25	26	27
53	28	29	30	31			

December – January

31 Monday

New Year's Eve
Hogmanay (Scotland)

1 Tuesday

New Year's Day
Holiday (UK, Republic of Ireland)

2 Wednesday

2 January holiday (Scotland)

3 Thursday

4 Friday

5 Saturday

6 Sunday

Epiphany (Christian)
New moon ●

Snowy scene *by Josiah Launstein*
Every year snowy owls arrive from further north to overwinter on the
Canadian prairies, near to where Josiah lives in southern Alberta. When this
male landed on a weathered old fence, he neatly captured the elegant bird in
its windswept environment.

January

7 Monday

8 Tuesday

9 Wednesday

10 Thursday

11 Friday

12 Saturday

13 Sunday

Dark snow *by Daniel Beltrá*
The ice sheet near Ilulissat, western Greenland, is peppered with black-dust
melt-holes and threaded with ribbons of blue meltwater. The black dust
consists of ash and soot blown by the wind. This black ice acts like a dark
curtain, increasing absorption of heat and the melt rate of the ice.

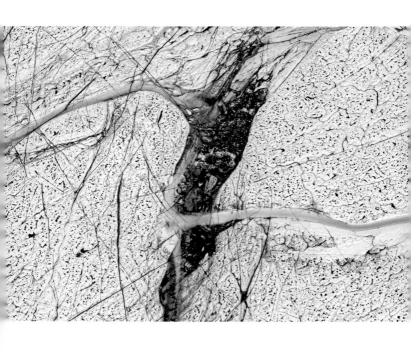

---

14 Monday

---

15 Tuesday

---

16 Wednesday

---

17 Thursday

---

18 Friday

| 19 Saturday | 20 Sunday |

By the light of the moon *by Audun Rikardsen*
At night, in a scene lit by the moon, a brown trout hangs in the shallows of
a river in northern Norway. Audun knows exactly when the fish congregate
and which bends of the river they favour, allowing him to get the image
exactly as he visualised it.

21 Monday

22 Tuesday

23 Wednesday

24 Thursday

25 Friday

Burns Night (Scotland)

26 Saturday

Australia Day

27 Sunday

Ice-cave art *by Floris van Breugel*
It was pitch black, cold and slippery as Floris squeezed into one of the many
lava-tube caves in California's Lava Beds National Monument. The darkness
hid a multitude of forms and colours within a layer of ice almost a metre
deep, which he was determined to photograph.

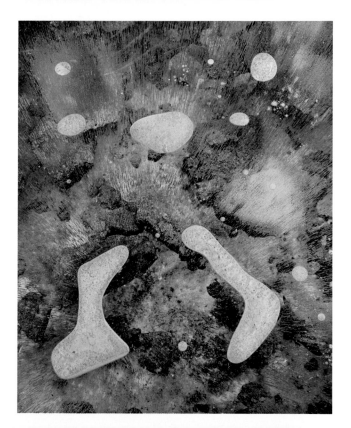

28 Monday

_____

29 Tuesday

_____

30 Wednesday

_____

31 Thursday

_____

1 Friday

_____

2 Saturday | 3 Sunday

Jagged peace *by Floris van Breugel*
While Floris was scouting for compositions in the backcountry of Argentina's
Los Glaciares National Park, a little bird showed up – a black-billed shrike-
tyrant. With fresh snow and muted light evoking the quiet wilderness, the
bird completed the shot.

4 Monday

5 Tuesday

Chinese New Year (Year of the Pig)

6 Wednesday

7 Thursday

8 Friday

9 Saturday

10 Sunday

Murmuration in the storm *by Andrew Forsyth*
Despite the severe storms that hit Brighton's coast in 2013, the starlings
continued to perform spellbinding aerial shows. Shooting directly into the
lashing rain, Andrew used the sea as a dramatic backdrop and captured
the traces of murmuring starlings, as if disappearing into the waves.

11 Monday

___

12 Tuesday

___

13 Wednesday

___

14 Thursday

Valentine's Day

___

15 Friday

___

16 Saturday

17 Sunday

___

Winter magic *by Etienne Francey*
Etienne had been itching to use his macro lens all winter. 'It opens the door
to the imagination,' he explains. He just hadn't found the right subject until
snowdrops appeared near his home in Fribourg, Switzerland. 'I love their
simplicity, and how they bloom so early, unafraid of the cold.'

18 Monday

19 Tuesday

20 Wednesday

21 Thursday

22 Friday

23 Saturday	24 Sunday

Landscape in ash *by Hans Strand*
Flying over southern Iceland's Fjallabak Nature Reserve in the highlands
of Landmannalaugar, Hans came across 'this magical place'. The icefields
and glaciers lining the flanks of the mountains were stained grey with ash,
recording in glorious textural detail the slow movements of snow and ice.

February – March

25 Monday

26 Tuesday

27 Wednesday

28 Thursday

1 Friday   St David's Day (Wales)

2 Saturday | 3 Sunday

A whale of a mouthful *by Michael AW*
An imposing Bryde's whale rips through a mass of sardines. Photographing
this feeding frenzy offshore of South Africa's Transkei (Eastern Cape) was
a real challenge. Already knocked clean out of the water by whales on two
occasions, Michael just managed to stay out of the way during this encounter.

4 Monday

5 Tuesday

Shrove Tuesday, Pancake Day (Christian)

6 Wednesday

Ash Wednesday (Christian)
New moon ●

7 Thursday

8 Friday

9 Saturday

10 Sunday

Coastal colours *by Jens Rosbach*
The intense turquoise of the sea off Fuerteventura in the Canary Islands,
contrasting with the sky and sand, inspired Jens to create this painterly
image. To produce the effect he used a 'camera in motion' technique
involving a long exposure and sliding a hand-held camera along the horizon.

11 Monday

12 Tuesday

13 Wednesday

14 Thursday

15 Friday

16 Saturday

17 Sunday   St Patrick's Day (Ireland)

The tunnel of spring *by Ugo Mellone*
Ugo had heard of a strange phenomenon in southern Spain's Sierra Nevada
– huge temporary snow tunnels forming as the meltwater runs off the peaks.
On discovering this hidden tunnel, Ugo found himself walking into a secret
oasis lined with lush grass and lit by natural skylights.

18 Monday   St Patrick's Day, holiday (Ireland)

19 Tuesday

20 Wednesday   Spring Equinox

21 Thursday   Full moon ○

22 Friday

23 Saturday   24 Sunday

The meltwater forest *by Fran Rubia*
There was magic in the mud. As Fran watched, invisible forces sketched a
picture on the ground. Meltwater from Iceland's Vatnajökull glacier, filtering
through the soil on a gentle slope, sent mud granules of a specific density
into motion until an entire forest had been created.

25 Monday

26 Tuesday

27 Wednesday

28 Thursday

29 Friday

30 Saturday

31 Sunday

Mothering Sunday
British Summertime begins, clocks go forward

Beetle beauty and the spiral of love *by Javier Aznar González de Rueda*
Javier was on the slopes of Ecuador's Tungurahua volcano when he came
across this dazzling pair of mating jewel weevils. It took him many attempts
to keep their tiny forms, just millimetres long, in focus as they travelled along
the plant's spiralling tendril.

April

1 Monday April Fools' Day

2 Tuesday

3 Wednesday

4 Thursday

5 Friday New moon ●

6 Saturday

7 Sunday

A black bear looks in *by Connor Stefanison*
When Connor spotted bear droppings near his camera trap in Maple Ridge
forest, British Columbia, his heart fell. Black bears are notorious for damaging
equipment. Relief turned to delight when he realised that he had an image
of the bear and that it was staring directly into his camera.

8 Monday

9 Tuesday

10 Wednesday

11 Thursday

12 Friday

13 Saturday

14 Sunday   Palm Sunday (Christian)

Still life *by Edwin Giesbers*
A great crested newt hangs motionless near the surface of the stream. Also
motionless in the water, in Gelderland in the Netherlands, was Edwin in a
wetsuit. He had very slowly moved his compact camera right under the newt,
turning the amphibian into a floating silhouette among the trees.

15 Monday

16 Tuesday

17 Wednesday

18 Thursday

Maundy Thursday (Christian)

19 Friday

Good Friday, holiday (Christian)
First day of Passover (Jewish)
Full moon ○

20 Saturday

21 Sunday

Easter Sunday (Christian)
Queen Elizabeth II's Birthday

Meadow canvas *by Klaus Tamm*
Returning to the spot where he'd seen some impressive lizard orchids, near
Greve in Tuscany, Klaus found the bulbs dug up and eaten. Turning, he
caught sight of two solitary, pink blooms in the meadow opposite, standing
out from a sea of vetch and other meadow plants.

22 Monday   Easter Monday, holiday (Christian)

23 Tuesday   St George's Day (England)

24 Wednesday

25 Thursday   Anzac Day (Australia, New Zealand)

26 Friday

27 Saturday   Last day of Passover (Jewish) | 28 Sunday

Mama's back *by Ashleigh Scully*
Ashleigh spotted the cubs romping about close to her cabin in Grand Teton
National Park, Wyoming. Creeping outside she started to photograph them.
After a while, their mother appeared, and the moment the cubs saw her,
they bounded over. 'There was so much affection between them,' she says.

29 Monday

30 Tuesday

1 Wednesday

2 Thursday

3 Friday

4 Saturday   New moon ● | 5 Sunday   Ramadan begins (Islamic)

Splash point *by Sheldon Pettit*
Rather than photograph the dramatic Hamersley Gorge itself in Karijini
National Park, Western Australia, Sheldon chose to illustrate the beauty of a
tiny waterfall, about 40 centimetres wide. He framed the picture as a square
so the impact of the water became central to the composition.

6 Monday

---

7 Tuesday

---

8 Wednesday

---

9 Thursday

---

10 Friday

---

11 Saturday | 12 Sunday

Wings of summer *by Klaus Tamm*
On an evening walk in Tuscany, Klaus discovered a meadow that was alive
with butterflies. A pair of black-veined white butterflies perched opposite
each other caught his eye. He used a wide aperture to blur the meadow
colours and then framed the butterflies against a window of sky.

13 Monday

14 Tuesday

15 Wednesday

16 Thursday

17 Friday

18 Saturday   Full moon ○ | 19 Sunday

Turtle flight *by David Doubilet*
As this hawksbill turtle swam past, David angled his camera and strobes to
illuminate the beautiful amber underside of the turtle. Framed by a backdrop
of barracuda and batfish, he used a slow shutter speed to capture it soaring
through its realm off Kimbe Bay, Papua New Guinea.

20 Monday

21 Tuesday

22 Wednesday

23 Thursday

24 Friday

25 Saturday

26 Sunday

Angle poise *by Marc Albiac*
Marc spotted this conehead praying mantis among the brambles in his
grandmother's garden in Barcelona. To show off the exquisite detail of the
animal, he taped a sheet of white paper behind it, which revealed the insect's
extraordinary shape, posture and behaviour in perfect portrait.

27 Monday   Spring holiday (UK, Scotland)

28 Tuesday

29 Wednesday

30 Thursday   Ascension Day (Christian)

31 Friday

1 Saturday   2 Sunday

Rhythm of the blues *by Cristobal Serrano*
On a trip to Faial Island in the Azores, Cristobal encountered these two blue
sharks with their attendant pilot fish. 'I especially wanted a view looking
down on them,' he explains, 'to illustrate the beautiful, sinuous movement
that characterises their elegant swimming style.'

3 Monday

June holiday (Republic of Ireland)
New moon ●

4 Tuesday

Ramadan ends (Islamic)

5 Wednesday

6 Thursday

7 Friday

8 Saturday

9 Sunday

Whitsun (Christian)

Waiting for the sun *by Edwin Giesbers*
Still drowsy from sleep, banded demoiselles wait for the Sun to heat
their bodies up so their aerial mating dance can begin. Edwin spent many
mornings at the same spot on the banks of his hometown river in the
Netherlands, watching them wake.

10 Monday

11 Tuesday

12 Wednesday

13 Thursday

14 Friday

15 Saturday

16 Sunday

Father's Day
Trinity Sunday (Christian)

Golden catch *by Thomas Villet*
'I wanted to capture this splendid bird in the most beautiful moment of the
day,' says Thomas. After digging a hide beside a lake in central France, he
waited each morning at dawn. On day four there was 'incredible light' and he
created this evocative picture of a great egret and its catch.

June

17 Monday
Full moon ○

18 Tuesday

19 Wednesday

20 Thursday
Corpus Christi (Christian)

21 Friday
Summer Solstice

22 Saturday

23 Sunday

Komodo judo *by Andrey Gudkov*
Two Komodo dragons wrestle along the majestic coast of Indonesia's
Komodo National Park. Andrey had visited many times, hoping to capture
the spectacular fights. On this trip, a confrontation escalated – the lizards
reared up on their hind legs, supported by their long, muscular tails.

June

24 Monday

25 Tuesday

26 Wednesday

27 Thursday

28 Friday

29 Saturday

30 Sunday

The heart of the swamp *by Georg Popp*
Despite his long career as a landscape photographer, Georg still believes
the cypress forests in Louisiana's Atchafalaya Basin are 'some of the most
beautiful places you have ever seen'. The 1,000-year-old cypress trees are
festooned with thick drapes of Spanish moss.

July

1 Monday — Canada Day

2 Tuesday — New moon ●

3 Wednesday

4 Thursday — Independence Day (USA)

5 Friday

6 Saturday

7 Sunday

To drink or not *by Carlos Perez Naval*
Western gulls were monopolising dishes of fresh water set out by locals for
the California ground squirrels. Carlos was fascinated by the way the squirrels
would sneak a sip when the gulls weren't looking. He managed to press the
shutter just before this gull lunged forward and the squirrel fled.

July

---

8 Monday

---

9 Tuesday

---

10 Wednesday

---

11 Thursday

---

12 Friday   Battle of the Boyne, holiday (Northern Ireland)

| 13 Saturday | 14 Sunday |

Flight of the scarlet ibis *by Jonathan Jagot*
Anchored in an estuary at low tide off the island of Lençóis on the coast of
northeast Brazil, Jonathan saw his first scarlet ibis. As the tide rose, so did the
ibis, creating a glorious pattern of scarlet wings against the canvas of sand
and tropical blue sky.

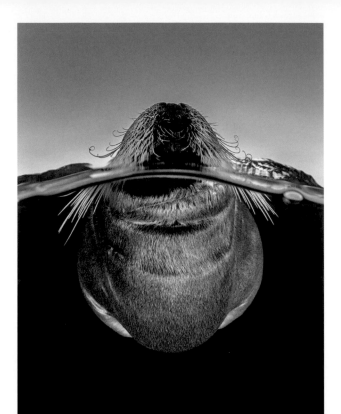

July

15 Monday

St Swithin's Day (Christian)

16 Tuesday

Full moon ○

17 Wednesday

18 Thursday

19 Friday

20 Saturday

21 Sunday

Deep sleeper *by Audun Rikardsen*
Late one evening, Audun received a call telling him that something strange
was bobbing around in a fjord outside Tromsø, Norway. Investigating by
boat, he found a visitor from the high Arctic – a bearded seal snoozing at the
surface, its distinctive whiskers dried into curls in the midnight sunshine.

22 Monday

23 Tuesday

24 Wednesday

25 Thursday

26 Friday

27 Saturday

28 Sunday

Cormorant cityscape *by Frank Abbott*
As the sun set on a salt marsh on Florida's Santa Rosa Sound, coastal birds
began to roost on the pier remnants, mostly double-crested cormorants,
plus the odd brown pelican and great egret. Tripod firmly grounded, Frank
increased the exposure to give the water an ethereal quality.

29 Monday

---

30 Tuesday

---

31 Wednesday

---

1 Thursday   New moon ●

---

2 Friday

---

3 Saturday	4 Sunday

Battle of the bee-eaters *by Juan van den Heever*
When Juan witnessed a fight between two southern carmine bee-eaters in
Katima Mulilo, Namibia, he challenged himself to capture the action. With
determination and a fast shutter speed, he managed it. These two males flew
at each other, using their bills to 'joust like fencers with swords'.

5 Monday

---

6 Tuesday

---

7 Wednesday

---

8 Thursday

---

9 Friday

---

10 Saturday | 11 Sunday

It came from the gloom *by Jordi Chias Pujol*
Jordi had just five minutes in the freezing cold waters of the Antarctic,
before facing decompression or hypothermia. He had time to capture
this *Atolla* jellyfish, lit by strobes in the dark, and when a group of gentoo
penguins zoomed across the frame he just managed to catch the last one.

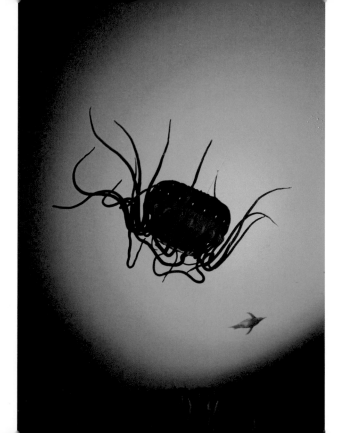

August

12 Monday

13 Tuesday

14 Wednesday

15 Thursday   Full moon ○

16 Friday

17 Saturday

18 Sunday

Realm of the flamingos *by Paul Mckenzie*
The winding monochrome patterns of Tanzania's Lake Natron provided
an enchanting backdrop when these crimson flamingos glided into shot.
The patterns on the lake are formed by sodium compounds, produced by
evaporation at the hot lake surface, reaching temperatures of 60˚C (140˚F).

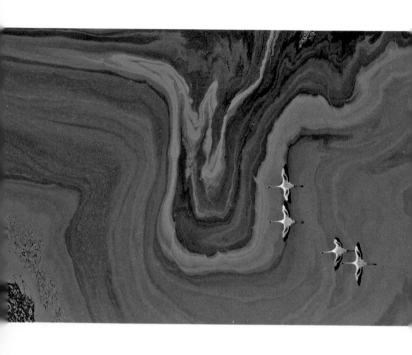

19 Monday

20 Tuesday

21 Wednesday

22 Thursday

23 Friday

24 Saturday

25 Sunday

Desert survivor *by Sergey Gorshkov*
Flying over the silky desert dunes of northern Namibia in 2013, Sergey
spotted many gemsbok – mostly dead, following the worst drought in the
region for a generation. When the pilot pointed out a live one, Sergey had
only seconds to capture the solitude of the hardy survivor.

August – September

26 Monday

27 Tuesday

28 Wednesday

29 Thursday

30 Friday

New moon ●

31 Saturday

1 Sunday

Natural frame *by Morkel Erasmus*
Peering out of a bunker beside a remote waterhole, in Namibia's Etosha
National Park, Morkel could hear every rumble, even smell the elephants. His
'dream moment' came when a mother elephant framed the shot with her
legs, just as her calf walked into view framing a giraffe.

2 Monday

3 Tuesday

4 Wednesday

5 Thursday

6 Friday

7 Saturday

8 Sunday

Shadow walker *by Richard Peters*
As Richard shone a torch into his garden in Surrey one night, a fox trotted past, casting a shadow. This gave him the idea for a photograph. On this particular evening, his neighbours switched a light on and he was able to capture the silhouette of this patrolling vixen.

9 Monday

10 Tuesday

11 Wednesday

12 Thursday

13 Friday

| 14 Saturday | Full moon ○ | 15 Sunday |

Entwined lives *by Tim Laman*
The only route for this young orang-utan to reach the fruits of the strangler
fig was to climb 30 metres up the plant's thick root, entwined around its host
tree. The backdrop is the rainforest of the Gunung Palung National Park, a
protected orang-utan stronghold in Indonesian Borneo.

16 Monday

17 Tuesday

18 Wednesday

19 Thursday

20 Friday

21 Saturday	22 Sunday

The art of algae *by Pere Soler*
The Bahía de Cádiz Natural Park on the coast of Andalucia, Spain, is famous
for its marshes, reedbeds, sand dunes and beaches. Pere was there for a
phenomenon, only visible from the air, when parts of the marshes burst with
intense colour, creating a rich tapestry of textures and patterns.

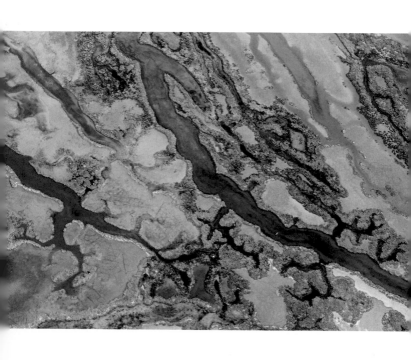

September

23 Monday   Autumn Equinox

---

24 Tuesday

---

25 Wednesday

---

26 Thursday

---

27 Friday

---

28 Saturday   New moon ● | 29 Sunday   Rosh Hashanah begins, Jewish New Year

---

Night of the mountain goats *by Connor Stefanison*
It was a clear, starry night, but with barely any moonlight framing the
mountain goats of British Columbia's Selkirk Mountains was guesswork.
Before attempting this shot, Connor had camped for three days, to allow
the goats to get used to his presence.

September – October

30 Monday

1 Tuesday   Rosh Hashanah ends

2 Wednesday

3 Thursday

4 Friday

5 Saturday | 6 Sunday

The company of three *by Amir Ben-Dov*
Amir spent many days observing the red-footed falcons, resting in Israel on
their way from eastern Europe to wintering grounds in Africa. Despite being
social birds, they tend to maintain a degree of personal space, but this male
and two females were often together, preening and touching.

October

7 Monday

8 Tuesday   Yom Kippur (begins in the evening) (Jewish)

9 Wednesday   Yom Kippur (ends in the evening) (Jewish)

10 Thursday

11 Friday

12 Saturday

13 Sunday   Full moon ○

The resurrected forest *by Ingo Zahlheimer*
An infestation of bark beetle destroyed vast areas of managed spruce forest
in the Bavarian Forest Biosphere Reserve in 1990. All logging was stopped. By
the time Ingo took this image, on a rainy day in autumn, nearly a quarter of a
century later, the forest had begun to rejuvenate.

October

14 Monday   Columbus Day (USA)

15 Tuesday

16 Wednesday

17 Thursday

18 Friday

19 Saturday | 20 Sunday

Cuban survivor *by Mirko Zanni*
Mirko always wanted to photograph the endangered Cuban crocodile, found
in the sinkholes of the Zapata Peninsula, western Cuba. Out of all the images
he took, this was the most special. 'I spent hours in the water with this one,'
he says, and at one point, 'it sank down right in front of me.'

21 Monday

22 Tuesday

23 Wednesday

24 Thursday

25 Friday

26 Saturday

27 Sunday   British Summertime ends, clocks go back
Diwali (Sikh, Hindu)

Pauraque study *by Jess Findlay*
Strictly nocturnal, the common pauraque rests by day, blending perfectly
with the surrounding vegetation. On a trip to Estero Llano Grande State Park,
southern Texas, Jess was thrilled to find one sleeping, and with a long lens
focused on the intricate markings of the bird's plumage.

October – November

28 Monday

29 Tuesday

30 Wednesday

31 Thursday

Halloween

1 Friday

All Saints' Day (Christian)

2 Saturday

3 Sunday

Frozen moments *by Hadrien Lalagüe*
Following a familiar childhood trail through the forest, Hadrien noticed this
unusual pattern of ice in a ditch, strewn with frosted oak leaves. Intrigued
by its formation he was drawn to capture its beauty. Balancing precariously
above the fragile surface he caught this moment of simplicity.

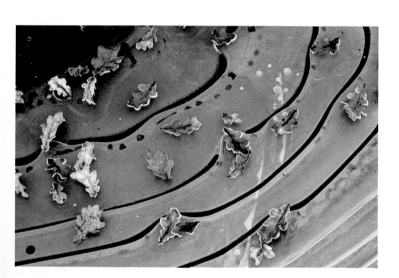

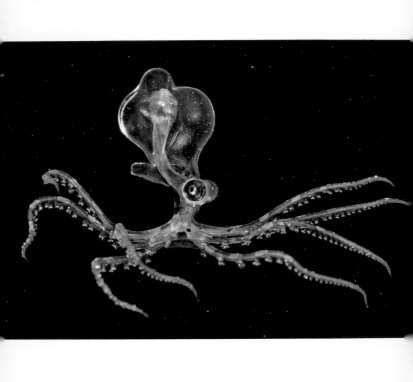

4 Monday

5 Tuesday
Guy Fawkes/Bonfire Night

6 Wednesday

7 Thursday

8 Friday

9 Saturday

10 Sunday
Remembrance Sunday (UK)

It came from the deep *by Fabien Michenet*
Fabien spends many hours diving at night in deep water off the coast of
Tahiti, French Polynesia. He is fascinated by the diversity of tiny creatures.
This juvenile octopus, just two centimetres across, 'stopped in front me,' he
says, 'waving its tentacles gracefully.'

11 Monday

12 Tuesday

Full moon ○

13 Wednesday

14 Thursday

15 Friday

16 Saturday

17 Sunday

Colours in ice *by Dag Røttereng*
On a trip to the Norwegian island of Smøla, following several cold days with
no snow, Dag found a pond with thick, clear ice, and seized the opportunity.
Looking for complementary colours, he ventured several metres out on to
the ice and found this pretty composition.

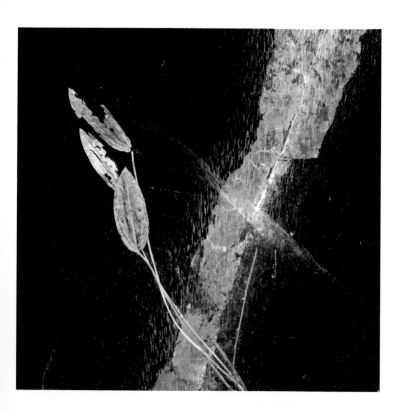

18 Monday

19 Tuesday

20 Wednesday

21 Thursday

22 Friday

| 23 Saturday | 24 Sunday |

A genet feat of a leap *by Marc Albiac*
Marc began leaving food out for the genets that visited the area near his
home in the Serra de Collserola, the mountains that rise above Barcelona.
Using a double exposure, he created a perfect portrait of this energetic
character, combining stars and poise as it hunted for rodents.

25 Monday

26 Tuesday   New moon ●

27 Wednesday

28 Thursday   Thanksgiving (USA)

29 Friday

30 Saturday St Andrew's Day, holiday (Scotland)	1 Sunday

Hot-spring skeletons *by Connor Stefanison*
Eerie skeletons emerge from the sulphurous steam of geothermal pools at
Mammoth Hot Springs in Yellowstone National Park. To create the ghostly
view of dead trees in the mist, Connor had to exclude the sky by standing on
a big rock to get the height, angle and perspective he needed.

December

2 Monday

3 Tuesday

4 Wednesday

5 Thursday

6 Friday

7 Saturday

8 Sunday

Dark dive *by Audun Rikardsen*
Herring shoals had started to overwinter in a fjord near Tromsø in northern
Norway, and where they go, humpbacks follow. Audun had located the
feeding group on a dark December afternoon by listening for their blows and
watching for their pale tail flukes in the polar night.

December

9 Monday

10 Tuesday

11 Wednesday

12 Thursday   Full moon ○

13 Friday

14 Saturday | 15 Sunday

Raven strut *by Connor Stefanison*
Thick, fresh snow covered the summit of Mount Hollyburn, which overlooks
Vancouver. The conditions at this popular lunch stop for hikers were ideal
for landscape photography, but Connor was there for the ravens. This one
landed in the perfect spot, displaying its characterful strut.

December

16 Monday

17 Tuesday

18 Wednesday

19 Thursday

20 Friday

21 Saturday

22 Sunday

Winter Solstice
Hanukkah begins, Festival of Lights (Jewish)

Snowbird *by Edwin Sahlin*
Cheese and sausage are what Siberian jays like, so Edwin discovered on a
trip to northern Sweden. Digging a snow pit deep enough to climb into and
scattering food around the edge, he was delighted when the jays flew right
over him, allowing him to capture the full rusty colours of their undersides.

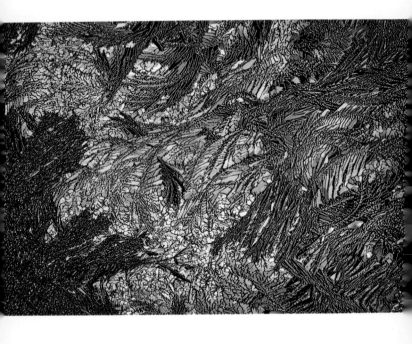

23 Monday

24 Tuesday

Christmas Eve (Christian)

25 Wednesday

Christmas Day, holiday (Christian)

26 Thursday

Boxing Day, holiday (Christian)
New moon ●

27 Friday

28 Saturday

29 Sunday

Angel wings *by Ellen Anon*
Temperatures in Pennsylvania had plummeted and Ellen woke one morning
to find ice inside one of her windows. Over the next few weeks, she
photographed the frozen patterns that came and went – here a golden
sunrise highlights the crystal formations in this intricate ice design.

30 Monday

Hanukkah, Festival of Lights ends (Jewish)

---

31 Tuesday

New Year's Eve
Hogmanay (Scotland)

---

1 Wednesday

New Year's Day
Holiday (UK, Republic of Ireland)

---

2 Thursday

2 January holiday (Scotland)

---

3 Friday

---

4 Saturday

5 Sunday

Scorched beauty *by Amy Gulick*
Amy photographed this scene 15 years after the largest fires in Yellowstone
National Park's history burnt more than a third of its forest, mainly lodgepole
pines. These trees are fire-dependent, producing cones that release their
seeds when subjected to fire. From destruction comes renewal.

Notes

Notes

Index of photographers

Week 51
Snowbird

Edwin Sahlin
Sweden
edwin97@comhem.se
www.edwinphoto.se
Nikon D7000 + 35mm f1.8 lens;
1/2000 sec at f7.1 (-0.7 e/v); ISO 320;
pop-up flash.

Week 17
Mama's back

Ashleigh Scully
USA
awscully12@gmail.com
www.ashleighscullyphotography.com
Canon EOS 5D Mark III + 500mm
f4 lens; 1/640 sec at f4.5; ISO 1250;
Gitzo tripod + Wimberley head.

Week 22
Rhythm of the blues

Cristobal Serrano
Spain
cristobal@cristobalserrano.com
www.cristobalserrano.com
Canon EOS 5D Mark III + 16-35mm
f2.8 USM lens at 16mm; 1/125 sec at
f7.1; ISO 500; Seacam housing.

Week 38
The art of algae

Pere Soler
Spain
pere.soler@outlook.com
www.peresoler.smugmug.com
Canon EOS 5D Mark III + 70-200mm
f4 lens at 70mm; 1/1000 sec at f5.6;
ISO 200.

Week 14
A black bear looks in

Connor Stefanison
Canada
connor_stef@hotmail.com
www.connorstefanison.com
Canon Rebel XTi + Tokina 12-24mm
f4 lens at 15mm; 1/200sec at f9; ISO
400; Trailmaster 1550-PS infrared trail
monitor; ×2 Nikon SB-28 and Nikon
SB-800 flashes.

Week 39
Night of the mountain goats

Connor Stefanison
Canon EOS 5D Mark II + 16-35mm
f2.8 lens at 16mm + Vello cable
release; 25 sec at f4; ISO 3200; Canon
430EX II flash; Gitzo GT3542LS tripod.

Week 48
Hot-spring skeletons

Connor Stefanison
Canon EOS 5D Mark II + 70-200mm
f2.8 IS lens at 200mm + B+W
polarizing filter + Vello cable release;
10 sec at f16; ISO 200; Gitzo
GT3541XLS tripod.

Week 50
Raven strut

Connor Stefanison
Canon EOS 5D Mark II + 16-35mm
f2.8 II lens at 16mm; 1/1000 sec at
f7.1; ISO 1600.

Week 8
Landscape in ash

Hans Strand
Sweden
strandphoto@telia.com
www.hansstrand.com
Hasselblad H3DII-50 + 50mm lens;
1/500 sec at f3.4; ISO 200.

Week 16
Meadow canvas

Klaus Tamm
Germany
tamm.photography@aol.de
www.tamm-photography.com
Canon EOS-1D X + 100mm f2.8 lens;
1/800 sec at f2.8 (+1 e/v); ISO 100.

Week 19
Wings of summer

Klaus Tamm
Canon EOS-1D X + 100mm f2.8 lens;
1/320 sec at f3.2 (+1 e/v); ISO 100.

Week 4
Ice-cave art

Floris van Breugel
USA
floris@artinnaturephotography.com
www.artinnaturephotography.com
Canon EOS 5D Mark II + 24-105mm
f4 lens at 45mm; 176 sec at f16; ISO
400; Gitzo tripod + Markins ballhead;
LED flashlight.

Week 5
Jagged peace

Floris van Breugel
Sony Alpha a7R + Nikon 14-24mm
f2.8 lens; 1/125 sec at f16; ISO 200.

Week 31
Battle of the bee-eaters

Juan van den Heever
South Africa
juan.heever@gmail.com
www.juanvandenheever.com
Nikon D4 + 200-400mm f4 lens;
1/4000 secs at f7.1; ISO 1000.

Week 24
Golden catch

Thomas Villet
France
thomasvillet@outlook.fr
Canon EOS 7D + 300mm f2.8 lens;
1/4000 sec at f2.8 (-1.7 e/v); ISO 100;
Manfrotto tripod; hide.

Week 41
The resurrected forest

Ingo Zahlheimer
Germany
ingo@zahlheimer.eu
www.ingozahlheimer-photography.de
Nikon D700 + 300mm f4 lens; 1/2500
sec at f4; ISO 1250.

Week 42
Cuban survivor

Mirko Zanni
Switzerland
mailto:mirkozanni.com
www.mirkozanni.com
Canon EOS 5D Mark II + 15mm f2.8
lens; 0.4 sec at f22; ISO 100; Seacam
housing; two Sea & Sea YS-250
strobes.

First published by the Natural History Museum, Cromwell Road, London SW7 5BD.
© The Trustees of the Natural History Museum, London 2018. All Rights Reserved.
Photographs © the individual photographers.
Text based on original captions used in the Wildlife Photographer of the Year exhibitions.
ISBN: 978 0 565 09455 3

All rights reserved. No part of this publication may be transmitted in any form or by any
means without prior permission of the publisher.
A catalogue record for this book is available from the British Library.
Printed in China by C&C Offset Printing Co. Limited.